Under Construction

Broken Pieces that Built Purpose

Tim Bo Mack

Www.truevinepublishing.org

Under Construction
Tim Bo Mack

Published by
True Vine Publishing Company
810 Dominican Dr.
Nashville TN 37228
www.TrueVinePublishing.org

ISBN: 978-1-968092-47-4 Paperback
ISBN: 978-1-968092-48-1 eBook

Printed in the United States of America.
For information, contact the author.

TABLE OF CONTENTS

DEDICATION

"To My Tribe…You know who you are.
Thank you for standing with me, believing in me,
and loving me through every season. I dedicate this
book to you."

INTRODUCTION
Still Under Construction

There's something sacred about the process of being built, the messy middle between who you were and who God is shaping you to become. It's not always pretty. It's not always fast. And it's definitely not always comfortable. But it's holy. Because when God begins construction on your life, He doesn't just rebuild what's broken, He reveals what's been buried.

I know this because I've lived it.

I was born and raised in a small town called Beeville, Texas, a place that taught me the value of hard work, faith, and family. My mother was a strong, determined woman who carried a quiet fire. As a kid, I thought her strength was anger. I thought she didn't like me, maybe even hated me. But later I learned the truth: she wasn't trying to hurt me; she was preparing me. She saw strength in me that I didn't yet see in myself. What I once thought was rejection was, in fact, preparation for the road ahead.

When my mother moved us to Houston for better career opportunities, I felt lost. I didn't fit in. I was bullied, misunderstood, and constantly felt like I wasn't enough. The city was supposed to be full of opportunity, but to me, it felt isolating. Eventually, I had had enough of trying to fit where I didn't belong, enough of questioning my worth. So during the second half of my junior year of high school, I moved back to Beeville to live with my grandmother. Her home became my steady, spiritual, and safe foundation. Her love helped me begin rebuilding my confidence and identity.

My father wasn't present much when I was growing up, and that absence shaped me more than I realized. But later, God allowed our paths to reconnect. Through forgiveness and grace, I found healing not just between father and son, but within myself. I learned that restoration is possible, even when you think too much time has passed.

After high school, I went on to study cosmetology in college. I was formally trained to transform my guests from the outside in, helping them look their best, feel renewed, and walk out of my chair with confidence. But over time, I realized something more profound: the fundamental transformation doesn't start on the outside. It begins within.

Every client who sat in my chair carried more than just hair; they had stories, pain, dreams, and silent battles. I began to understand that my hands weren't just gifted to style; they were anointed to serve. God had placed me in an industry of beauty not by accident, but by assignment. This is my divine calling: to touch lives through transformation, to remind people of the beauty within, and to help them see it reflected on the outside.

Life, however, has a way of testing even your faith and purpose. I was fired from a job I thought would define me, and what I thought was failure turned out to be divine redirection. That moment gave birth to what I now call my accidental business. What I saw as rejection was, in fact, God positioning me for purpose.

But the biggest construction zone wasn't my career. It was me.

I hit a season where my body, mind, and spirit were all in crisis. I gained a substantial amount of weight, which caused serious health challenges that almost killed me: two major epileptic seizures back to back, dangerously high blood pressure, and deep depression. For years, I had drowned my pain in heavy drinking. When I finally put down the bottle, I replaced it with food. Emotional eating became my comfort, but the weight I carried on my body reflected the weight I carried inside.

Those seizures were my wake-up call. My breaking point became my breakthrough. In that still, heavy place, I reconnected with the Holy Spirit. God reminded me that even when I thought I was broken beyond repair, He was still at work. I was being built piece by piece, layer by layer, into who I was always meant to be.

Today, I am still growing and still healing, still under construction. And that's the message of this book: healing, faith, and purpose are built one layer at a time. You don't have to have it all figured out to move forward. You have to keep building, even when it's messy.

Because sometimes, God has to break down what you built on your own so He can rebuild it the right way.

This is my story, but it's also a mirror for anyone who's ever felt lost, unworthy, or unfinished. It's for the ones still standing in the rubble of disappointment, trying to make sense of what's next.

I want you to know: you are not broken beyond repair. You are being rebuilt by design.

So welcome to the journey.

Welcome to the process.

Welcome to the CONSTRUCTION ZONE.

CHAPTER 1
Beeville Beginnings

Beeville, Texas, is a small town where everyone knows your name, your business, and sometimes your secrets. Growing up there, I learned early that life doesn't hand you anything; you have to work for it. And in that town, my mother was a living lesson in strength, discipline, and perseverance.

She was a woman with fire in her soul and hands that never rested. At the time, I didn't understand her. I thought her toughness was anger. I thought she didn't like me, maybe even hated me. I couldn't see the love behind the discipline. I only saw the pressure, the high expectations, and the moments when I inevitably fell short. I felt like I was constantly failing her, failing myself.

Looking back now, I see it clearly: she was preparing me. She saw strength in me that I didn't yet recognize in myself. What I mistook for rejection was, in fact, a lesson in resilience, independence, and faith. She wanted me to grow up strong because life would not coddle me. In her own way, she was showing me that God's love sometimes comes wrapped in challenge, not comfort.

Life in Beeville wasn't always easy, but it was real. The streets, the schools, the small neighborhoods, they taught lessons no classroom could. I learned early that kindness was mighty, but toughness was necessary. You had to stand up for yourself, even when the world seemed stacked against you.

Even with all the challenges, Beeville gave me roots, a foundation of faith, family, and hard work. My grandmother, whom I would later live with during a pivotal season of my teenage years, became my safe place. She was quiet, patient, and unwaveringly faithful. Her home taught me that love isn't always loud, but it's steady, consistent, and reliable.

Beeville also taught me that feeling "not enough" is universal, that even in a small town, you can feel invisible, misunderstood, and overlooked. Those feelings would follow me, challenge me, and eventually push me to discover who I truly was, not just who others thought I should be.

Looking back, every narrow street, every challenge, every hard lesson in Beeville was scaffolding. It was the first layer of my life's construction zone. And even though I didn't understand it then, I can now see that God was already at work, shaping me, molding me, and preparing me for the journey ahead. Beeville was small, but the lessons were big, and they would follow me, no matter where life took me.

The Move to Houston

When my mother moved us to Houston for better career opportunities, I thought it would be exciting, a fresh start, new possibilities, bigger dreams. But instead of excitement, I felt lost. The city was overwhelming, and I didn't fit in. The faces were unfamiliar, the schools were bigger, and the rules felt different. I was invisible in the crowd, and no matter how hard I tried, I couldn't seem to find my place.

Houston was supposed to be an opportunity, but for me, it became a battlefield and sometimes a prison. I was bullied, teased, and misunderstood. I carried the weight of feeling "not enough" everywhere I went, in the classroom, on the streets, even at home. I questioned myself constantly. Why couldn't I measure up? Why did everything feel so heavy?

It was a lonely season. I wanted to be anywhere but there, anywhere but me. I tried to fight to fit in, but the harder I tried, the more I felt like I was losing myself. Eventually, I had enough, enough of feeling like I didn't belong, enough of feeling like I wasn't enough.

During the second half of my junior year of high school, I decided to move back to Beeville to live with my grandmother. That move felt like returning to safety, a place where love was steady and patience abundant. Living with my grandmother gave me a new perspective. She didn't need to push me to be strong; she reminded me of who I already was. Her wisdom, her faith, and her quiet guidance became the anchor I desperately needed.

Back in Beeville, I began to reclaim pieces of myself that had been lost in Houston: confidence, identity, and purpose. I started to see that being "enough" wasn't about what others thought of me; it was about who God created me to be. And slowly, I began to trust that His plans for me were bigger than my struggles.

Looking back, the move to Houston, with all its challenges, was a turning point. It taught me resilience. It taught me patience. And it taught me that sometimes, God uses seasons of displacement and discomfort to redirect us to where we truly belong.

Beeville had given me roots, and Houston had tested them. Both were necessary. Both were building me. And in that construction zone, I was learning the first real lesson of my life: God is always at work, even when you can't see it.

Finding My Purpose

After graduating from high school, I was ready for a new chapter, a chance to turn the lessons I had learned in Beeville into something meaningful. I decided to go to college to study cosmetology. At the time, I thought it was just a career path, a way to earn a living and provide for myself. But God had bigger plans than I could see.

Cosmetology trained me to transform people from the outside in. I learned to cut, color, and style hair in ways that made my clients feel beautiful and confident. I loved the artistry, the creativity, and the ability to see a person walk out of my chair with a new sense of pride. But over time, I realized that the fundamental transformation didn't start with hair. It started within.

Every person who sat in my chair carried more than just hair; they had stories, struggles, dreams, and battles no one else could see. I began to understand that my hands weren't just skilled; they were a tool to serve and touch lives more deeply. God had placed me in this industry for a reason, not just to style hair, but to remind people of their worth, to restore confidence, and to reflect the beauty God had placed within them.

In those early years of my career, I began to recognize my divine calling. I realized that transformation wasn't just what I did for others, it was what God had been doing in my own life all along. Every challenge I had faced, every season of feeling "not enough," every struggle with identity and purpose, was shaping me to walk into this calling with empathy, understanding, and faith.

Looking back, I see how every step of my journey, Beeville, Houston, my grandmother's guidance, and my family dynamics all built the foundation for what was to come. God was teaching me the art of transformation, the power of service, and the importance of walking with faith, even when the process felt messy.

Cosmetology became more than a career. It became a ministry. It became a purpose. It became my first real lesson in what it means to serve with intention and lead with love. And just like my life, my calling was, and still is, under construction.

CHAPTER 2

The Father Factor

Unavoidable absences in life speak louder than words. Certain voids that shape you long before you even realize it. For me, that void was my father.

Growing up, I didn't have the luxury of a steady father figure. I had a man who shared my blood, but not my moments. Not my milestones. Not my memories. His absence didn't just leave a space; it built a lens. A lens through which I viewed myself, other men, and the meaning of being chosen, valued, and loved. When a father is missing, a child learns to fill in the blanks, and those blanks become beliefs.

For years, I wrestled with the quiet question that so many children of absence carry: "Was I not worth staying for?"

It wasn't a question I said out loud. It lived in the background, shaping my confidence, my expectations, and the way I approached relationships. When a father doesn't show up, a child often assumes something is wrong with them. And I was no different.

I learned early how to be strong. How to be independent. How to rely on myself. But beneath that strength was an unspoken ache, the ache of never having what every young boy deserves: someone to show him what manhood looks like, feels like, sounds like, and walks like.

I didn't hate him. I didn't even know him well enough to hate him. What I felt was more complicated than anger: absence. A presence that never existed. A space I normalized because I didn't know anything different.

But God knew.

The Reconnecting Season

There are moments in life when God circles us back to the places we tried to forget, not to reopen old wounds, but to finally heal them. My moment came later in life, when I wasn't looking for closure or reconciliation. I wasn't expecting anything. I wasn't demanding anything. But God knew what my heart needed before I did.

When my father and I reconnected, it wasn't dramatic. It wasn't some emotional movie moment with tears and apologies. It was real, raw, and human. Two men meeting again, no longer father and son, divided by years of absence, but two souls who needed a chance to rebuild what had been broken.

What surprised me most wasn't what he said. It was what I felt.

I felt peace.

Not immediately, not wholly, but gradually, like God slowly softening concrete that had been hardened for years. I realized something that changed everything:

His absence wasn't about me. It never was.

It wasn't my fault.

It wasn't my value.

It wasn't my fault.

My father's absence was a reflection of his wounds, his past, his brokenness, and his unfinished construction. Once I understood that, the anger lost its power. The questions lost their weight. And the child inside me finally exhaled.

Reconnecting with him taught me one of the greatest lessons of my life: Forgiveness isn't about giving someone another chance; it's about giving yourself a chance to heal.

The Healing Work
Healing wasn't instant. It wasn't tidy.

Healing looked like:

19

- Accepting the relationship for what it could be, not what it should have been
- Releasing expectations that were built on childhood fantasies
- Letting go of the need for a perfect apology
- Seeing him not as the man who wasn't there, but as the man who was trying now
- Choosing grace over grudges

Healing looked like God reminding me that every man has a story, even the ones who didn't know how to stay.

I learned to appreciate the small things: conversations, moments, attempts.

He wasn't perfect, but neither was I.

We were both under construction, building a relationship brick by brick, not rushed, not forced, just built.

Some people'll tell you it's too late, but I learned something different:

It's never too late for God to restore what time tried to steal.

Redefining Manhood

Growing up fatherless could have made me bitter. It could have made me hard. It could have built a man who didn't know how to love, lead, or express emotion. But instead, it made me intentional. It made me seek God in the places where a father should have stood. It made me hungry to break generational cycles, not repeat them.

Manhood, for me, was redefined through faith...not through the stereotypes of strength without emotion, toughness without vulnerability, or authority without compassion.

I learned that authentic manhood looks like:

- taking responsibility for your healing
- showing up even when it's hard
- leading with humility
- loving without fear
- forgiving without conditions
- being honest with your heart
- choosing your family every single day
- allowing God to shape the parts of you you've tried to hide

My father gave me a gift he never intended to provide: the determination to become the father I wished I had. And when my daughter was born, that lesson became my anchor. I wasn't just raising her... God was raising me.

The Redemption of a Father and a Son

Not every story gets a fairytale ending, but ours got a faithful one. Today, my relationship with my father isn't perfect, but it's present. Sometimes presence is the miracle. Sometimes showing up today is more

21

healing than all the years someone didn't show up before.

I learned to love him not for what he wasn't, but for who he is becoming. I learned to love myself beyond the shadow of his absence. Because forgiveness didn't just reconcile a relationship, it rebuilt a man.

CHAPTER 3
Love, Marriage & Grace

Love has a way of showing up exactly when you think you have everything figured out and exposing just how much growing you still have left to do. Marriage, even more than love, is God's way of refining you, stretching you, humbling you, and revealing the parts of you that would've stayed hidden if you lived life alone.

I didn't walk into marriage as a perfect man. I walked in as a man still learning himself and still healing. Still trying to understand what love looked like, felt like, and required. Then I met a woman who didn't just love me, she saw me.

The Gift of Partnership

My wife, Stephanie, became the mirror I didn't know I needed, the reflection that showed me both my promise and my flaws. She saw potential in the parts of me I used to hide. She saw purpose in my confusion. She saw strength when I felt weak. And she saw a husband in me long before I ever felt deserving of the title.

Partnership will test you in ways you've never been tested:

- Your pride
- Your patience
- Your communication
- Your willingness to listen
- Your willingness to grow
- Your ability to show up even when you don't feel like it

Marriage reveals the version of you that "singleness" could hide.

It exposes selfishness, inconsistency, and assumptions you didn't even know you carried.

But it also reveals your capacity to love, forgive, compromise, and evolve.

Stephanie didn't try to fix me...she covered me. She prayed for me when I didn't even have the words for myself.

She encouraged me when life tried to crush me. She loved me through seasons when I didn't feel lovable.

That kind of love? That's partnership.

That's grace.

Humility & Growth

Marriage taught me a truth I wish more men learned early:

Feelings do not sustain love; it's suffered by humility.

There were times I had to admit I was wrong. There were times I had to relearn how to communicate. There were times I had to unlearn habits shaped by childhood wounds.

And there were moments where the little boy inside me, the one who grew up without a father's guidance, had to learn how to be a man by the grace of God and the patience of my wife.

Growth isn't glamorous.

It's uncomfortable.

It's vulnerable.

It's intentional.

But marriage forced me to confront myself in ways nothing else ever had.

And it showed me that the best version of me wasn't built alone…it was built in partnership.

The Power of Commitment

Commitment is not just about staying...it's about choosing.

Choosing love when it's hard.

Choosing patience when emotions rise.

Choosing grace when pride wants the final word.

Choosing forgiveness when misunderstanding tries to steal the peace.

Commitment isn't always romantic.

Sometimes it's showing up even when you're tired.

Sometimes it's apologizing first.

Sometimes it's choosing unity over being right.

But commitment builds a foundation.

It builds trust.

It builds safety.

And it built a marriage that wasn't perfect...but was covered by purpose.

The Birth of My Daughter: A New Kind of Love

The day my daughter, Keily Arianna, was born, something shifted in me.

I held her in my arms, and for the first time, I understood what unconditional love felt like...not in theory, not in words, but in reality.

Looking at her small face, I felt a wave of conviction:

I wanted to be better.

I needed to be better.

I had to become the father she deserved.

Her tiny presence awakened something in me that I didn't know I had.

It healed parts of me that had been hurting since childhood.

It made me confront the gaps I still carried from my own father's absence.

And it pushed me to redefine manhood in a way that reflected God, not trauma.

Fatherhood became the most crucial construction zone of my life.

Not the kind where you build with your hands… but where you make with your heart.

I learned quickly that children don't need perfect fathers…

They need present fathers.

Fathers who show up.

Fathers who listen.

Fathers who love.

Fathers who try.

My daughter made me want to become the man I never had been, and the man God was calling me to be.

Grace in Marriage & Fatherhood

If marriage refined me, fatherhood reshaped me.

If partnership stretched me, parenting softened me.

If love humbled me, grace rebuilt me.

My wife and daughter became the greatest blessings I never saw coming…the tools God used to heal the wounds I never wanted to admit I had.

And through them, I learned this truth:

God doesn't just give you love…He gives you the people who help build you.

Marriage taught me commitment.

Fatherhood taught me responsibility.

Grace taught me patience.

And together, they taught me that the man I am today is not the boy I once was…because love has a way of transforming you from the inside out.

This chapter of my life didn't just teach me how to love better.

It taught me how to BE BETTER.

And the construction continues…

CHAPTER 4

Fired but Favored

When Breaking Feels Like Betrayal...but It's Actually Becoming

There are moments in life that don't feel holy when they happen.

They feel harsh.

They feel it is unfair.

They feel like God stepped away from the script of your life and left you on the stage alone.

Getting fired was one of those moments for me.

It didn't feel like "purpose."

It didn't feel like "divine timing."

It didn't feel like "all things are working together for my good."

It felt like rejection, with a final period at the end.

But here's the truth I didn't realize until later:

Some endings are God's loudest beginnings.

And some exits are heaven's way of removing you from a room that was too small for who you were becoming.

The Day Everything Shifted: The Unexpected Breaking Point

The day I lost my job, I lost more than a paycheck.

I lost a sense of identity.

I lost stability.

I lost the illusion of control.

And when a man loses control, insecurity rises and takes the wheel.

What will people think?

What am I supposed to do now?

How am I going to take care of my family?

Was I not good enough?

Did I fail?

In one moment, everything built on routine collapsed, and I felt stripped.

But sometimes, God has to strip you to rebuild you.

Not to shame you…

but to shape you.

That day didn't just break me.

It exposed me.

It revealed where I had placed my identity… in the job, not in the Giver of jobs.

Sometimes you need a holy disruption to remind you that your source is God, not the system.

The "accidental Business" That Was Actually an Assignment

I didn't plan to start a business. I didn't sit down with a five-step entrepreneurial strategy.

I didn't have investors, mentors, or a polished rollout plan.

Honestly? I didn't even know I was starting a business. I was trying to survive one day at a time.

But God had a different agenda.

I thought I was hustling.

God knew I was building.

I thought I was scrambling.

God knew I was stepping into purpose.

I thought it was temporary.

Heaven knew it was destiny.

When you're faithful, when you're willing, when you say "yes" to what's in front of you…God can take your little and multiply it into more than you imagined.

Looking back, I realized:

I didn't start a business…I stepped into an assignment.

An assignment that was bigger than income.

Bigger than schedules.

Bigger than services.

It was a calling to influence, uplift, sharpen, and shape people…inside and out.

It was purpose-dressed in the clothes of necessity.

It was a ministry disguised as work.

Sometimes you fall into what you were created for… accidentally.

But God doesn't do accidents…only alignment.

When Pain Becomes Your Push

When I lost my job, I didn't know I was stepping into something divine.

All I felt was the pain.

The pressure.

The fear.

The disappointment.

The embarrassment.

The weight of "What now?"

But pain is a teacher.

Pain pushes.

Pain purifies.

Pain positions you for what comfort would have kept you from.

If I had stayed comfortable…

If I had stayed secure…

If I had stayed in a job that didn't match my assignment…

I would have missed the version of me I was becoming.

That pain didn't just push me into purpose.

It forced me to grow.

It forced me to rely on God in a new way.

It forced me to stretch, think, create, believe, and move differently.

The place that hurt me became the place that birthed me.

Faith Over Fear: Trusting God With No Blueprint

Stepping into purpose without a plan is terrifying.

Stepping into purpose without savings is humbling.

Stepping into purpose without a guarantee is faith.

I didn't have answers, but I had obedience.

I didn't have clarity, but I had courage.

I didn't have a roadmap, but I had a relationship with the One who directs steps.

And somewhere between unemployment and uncertainty...

God showed me that faith is not knowing the whole path.

Faith is trusting the One who is the path.

During that season, I learned:

- God's provision doesn't always look predictable.
- God's timing doesn't always feel comfortable.
- God's plan doesn't always make sense until you look back.
- Fear is loud, but faith is louder when you feed it.
- Losing something doesn't mean God is losing control.

I didn't just get fired…

I got repositioned.

I got refined.

I got realigned.

I got pushed into a room I didn't know I was called to occupy.

I realized something powerful:

Being fired didn't break me…it built me.

And the favor that followed proved it.

The Favor That Finds You After the Fall

When God favors you, you don't need a title.

You don't need a corporate badge.

You don't need approval.

You don't need connections.

You don't even need certainty.

All you need is willingness.

And when you give God your willingness,

34

He gives you back a favor that doesn't make sense:

- Doors open without force.
- People show up without explanation.
- Opportunities find you without chasing.
- Success unfolds without striving.

The same season that embarrassed me elevated me.

The exact moment that humbled me, blessed me.

The same thing that looked like a loss became the launch.

I was fired…But I was favored.

And favor wins every time.

You Are Not Broken…you Are Built Differently

If you're reading this chapter and you've ever lost something you thought you needed, hear me clearly:

You're not being punished…you're being positioned.

You're not being rejected…you're being redirected.

You're not falling apart…you're falling into place.

Purpose usually shows up disguised as a problem.

But when the dust settles, you realize God wasn't breaking you…

He was building you.

And sometimes the only way God can get you to the next level
is by letting something fall apart at that moment.
I didn't know it then.
But now?
Now I see it clearly:
Getting fired didn't end my story.
It started the chapter that changed everything.

CHAPTER 5

Healing, Humility & the Holy Spirit

When Your Dark Place Becomes God's Construction Zone

There are places you fall into that don't look like a storm on the outside...but inside, everything is collapsing.

This wasn't heartbreak.

This wasn't a breakup.

This wasn't betrayal.

This was my dark place.

A place where I gained so much weight, physically and emotionally, that my body began to shut down.

A place where my health was in crisis.

A place where I didn't recognize myself in the mirror anymore.

A place where my spirit felt heavy, my confidence was cracked, and my hope was slipping through my fingers.

This wasn't sadness…this was survival.

And at the lowest point of that dark place…

My life almost ended.

The Day My Body Broke Down - the Wake-up Call

I didn't just gain weight…I gained consequences.

Silent ones.

Slow ones.

Deadly ones.

Two major epileptic seizures.

Back-to-back.

No warning.

No time to prepare.

No time to think.

One moment, I was standing.

The next moment, my world went black.

My blood pressure was so high that the doctors didn't understand how I was still alive.

My body was screaming for help, and I kept ignoring it for years.

My spirit was exhausted.

My mind was heavy.

My faith was quiet.

And the depression…

the deep, silent, suffocating depression…

was the heaviest weight of all.

I wasn't just at a breaking point.

I was at a life-or-death crossroads.

Some dark places are emotional.

Some are spiritual.

Mine was physical, mental, and spiritual…all at once.

When God Uses Darkness to Get Your Attention

I didn't understand it at the time, but that dark place was not punishment.

It was a pause.

It was a divine interruption.

It was God saying:

"If you keep going like this… You won't survive your own pace."

You don't forget the moment you realize you might not make it.

That kind of moment strips you.

It exposes everything you've been avoiding.

It reveals how fragile life really is.

It forces you to confront what you've been running from.

I had to face the truth:

I was hurting.

I was unhealthy.

I was ignoring myself.

I was drowning internally while showing up externally.

And the Holy Spirit met me there, not to shame me… but to save me.

The Holy Spirit: The Guide I Didn't Know I Needed

It didn't happen overnight.

For about a month and a half, I kept asking God to speak to me. I prayed. I questioned. I begged. I walked with Him early in the mornings because that was the only time I could disconnect from everything…when the world was quiet enough for me even to hope I might hear Him. Some mornings, I showed up desperate. Other mornings, I showed up tired. But I kept showing up.

And then one morning…He answered.

There were no fireworks. No dramatic signs. Nothing loud. His presence didn't crash in with thunder or lightning. Instead, it came gently… subtly…almost fragile enough to miss if I hadn't been paying attention.

It was so faint.

So quiet.

But it was holy.

"Shhhhh…"

That was it.

Not a speech.

Not an explanation.

Just a whisper.

But that whisper wrapped itself around my soul. It wasn't God silencing me…it was God calming me. It was the voice of a Father steadying His child. That "shhhhh" carried peace, comfort, authority, and love all at once. It said, You don't have to fight anymore. You don't have to figure it all out. Be still. I'm here.

And it broke me.

Tears filled my eyes, not from sadness, but from release. Something inside me finally exhaled. That whisper became the doorway…the moment my spirit finally quieted enough to hear Him truly.

From there, the Holy Spirit didn't come with noise…He came with awareness.

With conviction.

With compassion.

With clarity.

He helped me see:

- what I had been carrying emotionally that eventually showed up physically
- the stress and pressure that were slowly consuming me
- the pain I had buried instead of healing

- the habits that were silently destroying me
- the pride that kept me silent when I needed help
- the exhaustion hiding behind every "I'm fine."

And slowly, the Holy Spirit began reconstructing me from the inside out.

Not through shame.

Through grace.

Through truth.

Through alignment.

That dark place...what felt like the end... became holy ground. Because it was there, God began rebuilding the version of me that would truly live.

The Humility of Hitting Rock Bottom

There is nothing more humbling than your body telling you,

"We can't do this anymore."

Humility came in the form of hospital lights.

In the form of test results. In the form of conversations that forced me to face reality.

In the form of tears that came without permission. In the form of stillness I didn't choose.

Humility wasn't embarrassment. It was awakening.

Humility taught me:

- I needed help.
- I needed healing.

- I needed honesty.
- I needed God more than I needed image.
- I needed to stop pretending I was okay.
  The dark place didn't destroy me.

It broke the version of me that would have never survived the following season.

Surrender - the Construction Began With "yes"

You don't come out of a near-death experience the same way you went in.

But you also don't heal by willpower alone.

You heal by surrender.

Surrendering my habits.

Surrendering my pride.

Surrendering my pain.

Surrendering my coping mechanisms.

Surrendering the image of the "strong one" who never needs anything.

Surrender wasn't defeat...it was deliverance. Surrender was the moment God finally had full access to rebuild me correctly.

Because you can't ask the Holy Spirit to transform you

while holding onto the very things destroying you.

Surrender is not giving up...

It's handing over the tools.
So the Master Builder can take over the project.

The Rise From the Dark Place
I didn't just survive my dark place…
    I resurrected from it.
    The seizures didn't take me out.
    The weight didn't define me.
    The depression didn't swallow me.
    The fear didn't finish me.
    God stepped into my dark place
    and turned it into a construction site.
    The Holy Spirit rebuilt my discipline.
    Rebuilt my health.
    Rebuilt my mind.
    Rebuilt my faith.
    Rebuilt my identity.
    That season became my testimony.
    That pain became my purpose.
    That low point became my launching point.
    And today, I can say with boldness:
    My dark place didn't destroy me.
    It developed me.
    It delivered me.
    It deepened me.
    And it drove me back into the arms of God.
    Some people hide their dark places…

But I share mine and own it! Because it's the chapter that proves God still builds with broken pieces.

CHAPTER 6

Still Under Construction

You're Not Broken...You're Being Built

Here I am...not finished, not flawless, not perfect. Still growing, still healing, still learning. Still under construction.

If you've followed this journey with me, you know the truth: life isn't neat. It isn't linear. It isn't polite. Life will challenge you, push you, and sometimes break you. But God has a way of using every piece, even the broken ones, to build something greater than you ever imagined.

I've walked through small-town lessons, absence, love, loss, failure, and the dark place. I've faced rejection, fear, pain, and uncertainty. I've battled alcoholism, depression, health crises, and self-doubt. And yet, here I am.

Not because I'm perfect.
Not because I never fell.
Not because I had all the answers.
But because God never stopped building me.

Gratitude for the Process

There's a sacredness in the construction process…in the messy, imperfect, uncomfortable, and even painful seasons.

I am grateful for:

- The people who poured into me…My Tribe… who corrected me, and believed in me when I couldn't.
- The pain that taught me endurance, resilience, and faith beyond the easy days.
- The progress I can now see, layer by layer, like a building taking shape where there was once rubble.

Every setback, every challenge, every night of the soul… was a brick laid in the foundation of who I am today.

And I can say without hesitation: the construction was worth it.

Even when I wanted to quit. Even when the path seemed unclear. Even when I thought I was broken beyond repair.

God's hands were at work.

The Message for You

If you are reading this and you feel unfinished, unworthy, or lost...hear me:

You are not broken.

You are not behind.

You are not a mistake.

You are under construction.

Every season you walk through, every trial, every failure, every moment of doubt...

It is shaping you. It is refining you. It is teaching you faith, patience, humility, and perseverance.

Sometimes, you feel like rubble.

Sometimes, you feel like a mess.

Sometimes, you feel like you'll never get it right.

That's precisely when God is at work.

That's when He's building, layering, and preparing you for the next level.

That's when your breakthrough is quietly forming, even if you can't see it yet.

Moving Forward With Faith

I am still growing.

Still learning.

Still under construction.

And I'm okay with that.

Because I know God isn't finished with me.

I don't have to have it all together. I don't need every piece of the puzzle in place.

I have to keep building, keep walking, keep trusting, and keep surrendering to the One who designs the blueprint.

If you are in a rebuilding season, I want you to know:

Your dark place can become your launching pad.

Your failures can become your foundation.

Your struggles can become your testimony.

Your process is your purpose.

You are being built, and the masterpiece God is creating is worth every moment of discomfort, every layer of growth, and every step of faith.

Final Words

So, wherever you are in your story…whether you are starting over, still healing, or stepping into a new season, remember this:

You are not broken.

You are not defeated.

You are being built.

And when God is building, the result is always greater than the pain, the struggle, and the wait.

Stay faithful. Stay patient. Stay obedient.

Keep laying each brick with intention.

Keep trusting the process.

Because the best version of you is still being constructed!